MW01535372

How can I have fun making good things happen, even if I'm only a teenager?

A Youth Leadership Guide

Cedargrove Mastermind Group

ISBN-13: 978-1546934004
ISBN-10: 1546934006

Dedication

This book is dedicated to all the leaders that have helped me, to all the leaders that will benefit from this, and to the as yet unborn, who will inherit whatever great things, and messes, that we leave for them. This book is dedicated to those many leaders that make things happen, including Sharon, who trained teen leaders in my own community, and Christina, and Maria.

Those who say it is impossible need to get out of the way of those who are doing it. -Chinese proverb

Lead, follow, or get out of the way. -U.S. Marine maxim

It can be done, and we can have fun doing it.

If you think you can, or can't do it, you're right either way. -Henry Ford.

Look around you, right now. Every human creation you see was transformed, by someone guided by leaders, according to the pictures in their minds, of what was possible.

Be like water. If you can't get through an obstacle, go under it, or around it, or over it. If you can't do that, dissolve yourself, and fall into the other side- just like electrons get through impossible barriers, in quantum tunneling diodes. Your vision of what's possible can drill through anything, to become real, if you help it.

What if all you had to do, was hoist the sails of clear intent, and a strong wind just blew you to your goal, almost effortlessly?

Do something to help your goals along, every day. It feels so much better to light one candle, than to curse the darkness. Others may light lamps, with your candle.

Table of Contents

If it's worth doing, it's worth doing badly, to get the experience.

If it's worth doing, it's worth doing well, for the sheer joy of it.

There is do. There is not-do. There is no try. -Yoda, quoting Chinese philosophers

The one quality all successful people have is persistence. They just keep at it. They may try new approaches, but they never give up.

What if what you seek to create desperately wants to work with you, to come into being?

What if the Universe is already desperately trying to help you, right now, just as the ocean was helping Moana?

What kind of community would you like to live in, and enjoy, for the rest of your life? What does your heart tell you about this?

What kind of community would you like for your children to grow up in? And their children? And the unborn, that you will never see?

What would your community be like, if it were a wonderful place to live? Perhaps even better than the best you can imagine?

What would you see, hear, feel, and know, in this place?

How would you enjoy interacting with people?

How would the old teach the young? How would the young teach the old?

How would the young be trained early, to seek out their mission and purpose in life, and supported in accomplishing it?

How would people use intuition to deal with problems before they came up? How would people use intuition to anticipate economic shifts, and adapt to them well in advance?

If you knew that you would experience everything that you do to and for others, as them, feeling all the pain- or joy- that you put in their lives, how would your life change?

If you knew that everything you do to others, whether kind or cruel, would be passed on a few billion times, as it will, would you choose kindness, or cruelty?

What would it be like, to live a life full of peace, joy, love, prosperity, bliss, accomplishment, and all that makes life worthwhile, in a community that offers this to all?

Introduction

What is a leader? A leader is someone who gets things done. A leader begins with leadership of self. A leader identifies a useful goal, figures out the first step on that path to that goal, and takes it. A leader then evaluates, asks questions, identifies the next step, and takes it. You don't have to know the entire path, or even what the goal will be, precisely. It is possible to drive across country, seeing only the 60 feet/20m in front of your headlights, follow the signs on the road, and get to the other side of the country.

It is useful to have a completely defined goal. At the same time... you might find yourself going down another path entirely, to a different goal, that is much better. Leaders go with the flow.

There is a Chinese story about being a leader. Once upon a time, a woman on a boat was taken by pirates. The pirate ship wrecked, and she made it ashore. She took shelter among woodworkers that made spars for boats. She was able to take a boat home, but it also wrecked in a storm. She took shelter among ropemakers, who taught her that craft.

In time, she took another boat to go home, but she ended up in a typhoon, and ended up on yet another shore. This time she took shelter among people that made tents, of canvas. She learned how to weave canvas, and sew it. Then some nomads rode in, and kidnapped her.

She was sold to the court of the King of China. The King of China had a major problem- his kingdom was threatened by foreign forces, and he had to move his troops quickly. The troops needed shelter, on the move, but there were no houses or barracks for them. The woman thought, and an idea came to her. She went to the King, and said she had an idea.

The King was very interested. Desperation makes selling ideas easy. She told the King she could make a house- of canvas, held up by poles, using ropes to steady it. She made tents. The King was so impressed with this solution that he made her a queen.

See the pattern? She took her experience, and put different existing elements together in a new way. This is how almost all problems are solved. Leaders are very observant- and constantly reading, so they have new "spare parts" to play with, to creates solutions.

Henry Ford visited slaughterhouses in Chicago, and saw how cows were taken apart, into their parts, very quickly and efficiently. He turned the process around, to make the first assembly line, to manufacture cars. The wooden boxes used to ship cars had very precise specifications- because after they were unscrewed, the wooden pieces became floor boards in his Model T Fords. Both of my grandfathers drove Model T's.

Leaders are not leaders because of age, wealth, position, intelligence, or any other quality than that they see a problem as a growth opportunity, and study it until a solution downloads to their mind. It may only be a step on the path to the solution.

Many community leaders will deny they are leaders. They will say that they just did what needed doing. Here's an easy way to be a leader: use the above, and fake it till you make it. Pretend you are a leader. Anyone who would challenge you would be a leader themselves. No, most people prefer to follow. And once you have followers, and are getting things done, aren't you a leader? You are. It really is that simple.

Parents of children, over 30 or so years of age, suddenly realize that nice things happen in their communities because people make them happen. Their sense of mission and purpose in life has already expanded beyond their skin, because they have children.

Somehow, their sense of self encompasses the whole community. That is maturity. I have seen a few teenagers like this, however it seems that some teenagers need to get the whole partying thing out of their system, first.

When I was ten years old, I had access to my father's Scotch whiskey, and Gin. I decided I didn't like how they made me feel. So I stopped drinking alcohol. It wasn't useful. I had the opportunity to smoke cigarettes, later. They made me cough. Pot was everywhere, when I was in college. All I had to do was look at the people smoking it, and ask myself if I wanted to be like them. I didn't. Why not let someone else set off the mines?

There used to be a woman in my apartment complex, with kids. She had an issue with heroin addiction, as did her boyfriend. I could literally see them decaying, before they were evicted. Opiods hold no attraction for me. I got a video game on a 386 computer I had, some years ago. After going to work with an hour of sleep, one day, I realized I was addicted. I quit video games. They aren't useful to me.

The main reason that I can see for addiction is that people have a lot of pain, and they are self-medicating. The biggest reason for this pain seems to be that communities are fragmenting. Cornell West's book *The War on the Family* notes that communities were formerly far more mutually supportive than they are now. They provided a protective layer, for everyone.

I have spent time learning everything I could from Native American elders. They see the same things in their communities. They do all they can to inspire their young, to expand their sense of self outside of the small self, to follow their mission and purpose in life, to grow in awareness, and to grow into who they truly are. In my perhaps small way, I offer this book, to do the same thing. Books have become our elders.

I have a daughter in her early 30's. I got custody of her when she was four years old, and raised her. Actually I didn't raise her, she told me what she needed, here and there, and occasionally shared with me bits and pieces of her life. She was very self-directed.

I knew that the only lesson I could ever teach her was that *decisions have consequences*. She figured that out. There was a guy in her class, who was truly gifted with the guitar, I mean so good he could have been nationally known. He drank so much alcohol that by the age of 23, he couldn't play the guitar any more. His nervous system was shot.

I took my daughter to a funeral, for someone in her high school. This 17 year old was in an auto accident. Four kids were in a car doing 70 miles per hour, on a dirt road. They didn't make a curve, and hit a tree, sideways. Two of the kids didn't make it. The other two were hurt, but survived. One was the driver. I wonder how she felt.

Decisions have consequences. The hardest part about being a parent is that children do not listen- they imitate. That is some serious discipline. My older daughter embodies my values better than I do. She finished college faster than I did, with higher grades, she had more friends, and more fun, and she got to go to graduate school. She married far better than I did, and she has a great kid. I remember when I saw her born. The sudden feeling realization came over me, that I couldn't do stupid things any more. A young child was dependent on me. *Choices choose futures, and decisions have consequences.*

When you consider doing something- look first to someone who has done it for a while. Then ask yourself- is that where I want to be, five-ten years from now? Look at alcoholics, addicts, and so on. They are teachers. They offer lessons, for the aware, every day. What kind of lessons will you offer to others? No matter what you choose to do, you will offer lessons by your example.

Embody your Vision of your Life

We suggest reading this slowly, in a very relaxed state.

I BURN BRIGHT with the power and force of my Vision

I find a way to use everything: every letter, every word,

Every conversation, every meeting, every chance encounter

Every hobby, fascination and passion and skill and gift and word

To CRYSTALLIZE MY VISION to

BECOME and BE the TRUTH I want to see in the world

I: model it- glow with it- vibrate and resonate to it- play in it

I network addictively and effortlessly and playfully

Through energy feeling thought action love smiles kindness

I network from the truth, the Vision, deep in my soul

I am the Center, the Nest, the Sun of my Vision

The mantle for the Flame of my Truth

I am a free, effortlessly powerful welling of life,

Light, love, truth, and sparkling, harmonious, joyful, healing beauty

I feel it deep within my being

I know it to be true- for it is

I affirm it, project it, radiate it in concentric rings, light up my world

I enflame myself with its energy, its feeling, its vibration, its light and the miracle of the beauty, purpose, and truth of my own life manifests

As I help others realize their dreams

I realize my own

Great corporations, governments, the media, all seem so powerful

They are paper tigers, and parasites

Before the power of vision and networking, and they know it

Networking a Vision is the healing salve, the quintessence, the elixir of joy, Aladdin's lamp

It is freedom, the joy of creating, power to help others and self, democracy realized

Happiness, beauty, bliss, contentment, ecstasy, joy, love, peace, purpose in life, truth, satisfaction, the spiritual side of life

are all different faces of the same thing

and Vision crystallized through networking is the path

Things are only useful as a way to help me realize peak experiences

All great human creations started out as a feeling in the heart of one person

who persisted at bringing it into form

Where is my joy today? What is it telling me to be/do/have?

- Michael Patterson, used with permission

I. Setting the stage: you can do far more than you thought

Dr. Richard Feynman was a Quantum Physicist, who among other things, was on the team that created the first atomic bomb, during WW II. He said that the Observer is everything, because the Observer creates[1]. I grew up with Newton's Physics, which is the physics of the material world. If you design a bridge, you will need Newton's Physics. However, Newton's Physics are only a model.

Here is one example. If you stare at the back of someone's neck, for a minute, with total concentration, they will turn around, to see who is watching them, assuming they are awake, and sober. If you keep staring, they will meet your eyes. Have you ever "felt" someone watching you? That is not possible in Newton's Physics, because there is no action at a distance, except gravity. Yet still it happens. It works even through binoculars.

Have you ever been around someone who could only see your bad points, your shortcomings? Didn't you just want to get away from them, as quickly as you could? And then there was the person who could only see your good points, your potential, and just smiled. Didn't you just want to bask, and enjoy that attention?

Another way to say this, is that energy flows where attention goes, and what you concentrate on grows. If you have the ability to read this book, you have the ability to create, with observation. Certain kinds of questions can be very powerful, because they refocus attention, and observation. Most scientific discovery, and all new ideas, come into being because someone asked a new question.

---

1 He said that the Twin Slit experiment, in Quantum Mechanics, was enough to derive all of Quantum Mechanics from. I like playing with Quantum Mechanics, but I don't understand any of the mathematics. The basis of the Twin Slit experiment is that light responds to human expectation, or intent- to human observation. That is revolutionary.

What are my gifts, strengths, and abilities?

How much fun do I have, when I work from my abilities, gifts, missing and purpose in life, and strengths?

How does helping others develop my own abilities, and make me more alert, aware, and creative?

What are my top five values? How am I living my life, in respect for those values?

What is on my "bucket list", the list of everything I want to do in my life? What would I like to add?

In the military, when one retires, or gets out, one has to "clear", or return all equipment, and get a signature that everything has been returned. When I "clear" my life, at the end of it, what do I want to look back on?

What will my proudest accomplishments be?

What kind of kindness did I put in people's hearts?

How did I cheer people, and put joy in their lives?

How much fun did I have, and how did I help others have fun?

How else could I use questions, to develop my and others?

II. Guiding and directing the flow of change in life

Computers are useless. They can only give you answers. - Pablo Picasso

How does positive change happen? Someone makes it happen, or at least pushes it some. Why does that person decide to do that? They look at what is, and <u>start asking questions</u>. Here is one sequence:

1. *What would this be like, if it were better, more effective, or perfect?*
2. *What is missing, from the way it is now? Or, what would it have, if it was better, more effective, or perfect?*
3. *How could I have fun doing anything, however small, to get on the path, towards making that happen?*
4. *What is blocking, or stopping this from happening?*
5. *How can I have fun working around that?*
6. *How can I lay out all the pieces or steps, and ask people to help me, with one piece that they could help with?*
7. *Whom could I ask to help me, that would enjoy helping to make this happen?*
8. *How can I ask them, today, in a way that sets them on fire with the possibilities?*
9. *How can I keep doing this, examine my results, change what I'm doing or learn more, as necessary?*
10. *How would it feel, if this was already done? [This trains my nervous system in success; Olympic athletes do this, and I can, also.]*
11. *How can I do what I'm doing, in the excitement of the feeling of it already being done?*
12. *How would I celebrate each small victory on the path?*
13. *What else could I be, do, have, or know, that would help me?*
14. *How could I talk people into giving that to me, or to whoever is doing that piece?*
15. *How else could I have fun creating this?*

Apache [Indeh] scouts filled their minds with one question. I have to translate that question into two questions, to get the full range of meaning. Those two questions are:

1. *What is going on here?*
2. *What is this telling me?*

When you ask a question, you will get an answer. Here is the secret: *STAY IN THE QUESTION*, *not in the answer.* Why? Because you get a continuous stream of awareness, and noticings, when you stay in the question. This is very useful.

Part of staying in the question is staying out of judgement. The Chinese book *Hsin Hsin Ming* is a whole short book, on the important of staying out of judgement, so you can see what is going on. If you judge people, you limit their possibilities.

Nobody likes being judged. The book *Building Communities from the Inside Out* tells the story of a man that didn't talk, or do much. A community organizer knew that he had gifts, strengths, and abilities, as everyone does. She saw a bowling ball in his space. She asked if he liked to bowl. He did. She was able to connect him with a bowling alley, and then, to the larger community. He began talking again.

That is a useful story. Everybody has abilities, awareness, gifts, strengths, and so on. As you ask questions like those above, you will begin to be aware of this, and you'll start asking people whom they know, with some ability.

There are people in every healthy community, who collect data on people's strengths, and what gives them joy. When they see a possibility, where that person's gifts would fit in, they ask for help. Would you respond to a request, on how you could experience joy, using a gift you had? You probably would. When you start doing this regularly, it is almost like weaving a basket-you take weak reeds, or vines, and weave them together in a way that is mutually supporting, and end up with a strong basket, which is stronger than the sum of the strengths of the parts- because each part works together, in a larger whole.

I see more women than men doing this, and we'll talk about that later. Native Americans in the northern hemisphere say they learned how to be civilized by watching wolves. Wolves have three main roles, in the pack. There are scouts, there are leaders, and there are supporters. Wolves have strengths in one area. If one role is missing, another will fill in, if not as well.

I have a friend who lived with wild wolves, and hunted with the pack. The pack accepted him. There are many stories of humans raised by wolves. There is a movie, *Tierra de Lobos*, made in Spain, about a man who, as a boy, was dropped off in the woods to die, by his parents. A wolf pack took him in, and he lived with them, as a wolf. After some years, the Guardia Civil caught him, and reintroduced him to society. The movie scenes were made from this guy's memories. It is fascinating to watch, though one would need to know Spanish.

This is basic Systems Theory. The real being is not the wolf; it is the pack. The real being is not the human, it is the community. The maximum human "pack" size is about 150 people. This is the size of a company, in the Army, and even the employees at a Gore-Tex factory. That is all the people you can know well.

Albert Einstein was once asked how he would solve a difficult problem, if he only had 60 minutes. He said he would spend the first 59 minutes clearly defining the problem [using questions], and only then, act. This is very useful. If you do what you always did, you get the results you always got.

A manager tells people to cut the jungle growth faster. A leader climbs a tree, realizes the group is going in the wrong direction, and tells them to cut a path to the left, so they can travel on the open ground, and go faster. This shows that the most important thing is asking the right questions.

<u>People are the crystallization of the questions they ask</u>. I know you've seen people who ask how they can do as little as they can, and still get by. Their lives are not interesting. The people who are asking interesting questions- like how they can do more, how they can follow their bliss, how they can find the joy in what they are doing- lead far more interesting, and fun, lives. Often, the answer will show up as soon as you ask the right question.

A single question can change your whole life. An entrepreneur remembered being back in high school, visiting another class with a friend. The teacher asked what his burning dream was. He said he could never achieve his dreams, because he was "educably mentally retarded". The teacher asked, *"So, do you really want to let someone else's labels limit your life?"*

There are people who ask questions that are not useful. They might ask, "~~How come I'm so fat/stupid~~?" These are not useful questions. Neither are questions like these:

> ~~How come nobody cares about my problems?~~
> ~~How come other people get the good stuff, and I don't?~~
> ~~What the heck is wrong with other people/me?~~
> ~~Why can't I ever get what I want?~~
> ~~Why does bad stuff happen to me?~~
> ~~Why does it never work out for me?~~

A much better question would be *"How come I feel so energetic, when I think about my exciting goals?"* Feel the difference.

Let us recall that questions focus awareness- and observation. Your subconscious mind is an answer-finding mechanism. If you ask these questions, you will get answers. They just won't be useful. How is it useful, to be asking questions, where the answers aren't useful? You see, these questions focus attention, and creative energy, on what's wrong, and expand what is wrong. They constrict your possibilities, lower your energy level, and so, are not useful.

Now that we know that questions are always answered, **_why not ask questions where the answers would be useful_?** The ability to ask focused questions is more useful than the answers. Here's why. When you ask focused questions, you send your subconscious mind on a search, far outside of your usual limitations. It will keep seeking, until it finds the answer, or you stop the search.

Sometimes the answer shows up as you ask the question, as if it was just waiting for you to open the door, so it could get in.

How might having useful answers change your: ability to get things done, academic success, business, dealings with others, energy level, health, how you feel about yourself, love life, success, wealth, and every other area of your life?

What is your mission and purpose in life? Here is some help- mission always involves service to others, and joy is usually the road sign- there is some joy in doing it, for you.

Here are some useful questions you might start with:

If a leprechaun, who had no idea what adjectives were, described this situation, what would s/he say?

How have others had fun solving similar problems?

What do I feel really good about, in my life, in this moment?

What is the useful lesson in this challenge, crisis, disaster, growth opportunity, quarrel, problem, situation, or whatever else is happening here?

What is this telling me? What is really going on here?

What would Bugs Bunny do?

Where is my joy, here, and how can I follow it?

Where is the gift of awareness for me, in this situation?

Who would enjoy helping me shift this situation, in a fun way?

How would I feel, if this issue was already solved, in a way better than the best I can imagine?

Notice how each of these questions expands you, improves your energy, opens up possibilities, and generally just feels good. Maybe, like me, you have trouble interacting with people. I often have no idea what to say, and I have to deal with many people, every day. Here is a very simple solution to that issue:

What would an expert in this field say?

What would the smartest person who ever lived do?

Native Americans never answered questions completely. They answered questions only sufficiently to maintain interest, knowing that people would seek out their own answers, which would often be better than anything they could have said.

I wonder what questions I might ask of someone, that would wake them up to their mission and purpose in life, connect them to their hearts, and energize them to seek out that which is better than the best they can imagine?

How much fun could that be for them? And for me?

III. You don't get what you don't dream of, and ask for

Surveys show that Americans are more afraid of speaking in public than they are of dying. This is bizarre. I do some public speaking as part of my job, and also sometimes for fun. The first time I did public speaking, I was really bad. Well, I learned from my mistakes, did it some more, and got better. Now I enjoy it.

- *How can I feed people's interests, with what I'm saying?*
- *How can I get people laughing, here and there, as I focus their attention on something funny?*
- *How can I share my excitement about my subject?*
- *How does my subject let people in my audience achieve their dreams, and goals, as it puts joy in their lives?*
- *What would my audience enjoy learning about my subject?*

My sister, and daughter, say that I match the profile for Asperger's Syndrome, which is sort of high functioning autistic. My father probably also matched this, as did his father. I did first and second grade in one year. I could have graduated high school at 16, I had the academics, but did so instead 2 months after turning 17. I went to college. But I had no idea how to deal with people, beyond the most basic skills.

When I was in high school, people like me were "wierd", and the treatment was harassment. Well, ok. I did my fourth year Arabic final over 28 continuous hours, with no chemical help, due to my work schedule. I worked full time, as I went to college full time.

My M.A. thesis is 332 pages long, a translation of a history of Afghanistan. I needed five foreign language dictionaries, a Quranic concordance in Arabic, and various other references, to do it. I did it as a single parent, with custody of a four year old child, in the U.S. Army. I focused totally on my goal, and did what was necessary, to make it happen. More than 30 metaphorical doors opened up, on my path, that I thought were impossible to open.

My father's father died when he was 15. He finished high school in three years, and finished a four year degree in 2.5 years, working full time to pay his way, as there was no financial aid back then. It was the height of WW II, he knew he would be drafted, and he was motivated. He focused on his goal, and made it happen. As it turned out, he wasn't drafted, though many in his high school class were.

My father's father came off the farm at 21, with six years of schooling. He managed to get his doctorate, and taught in a college for 29 years. This was not easy, at that time, and wouldn't be now. He focused on his goal, and made it happen. The journey of a thousand miles begins with the first step, and continues, step by step by step.

Each of us didn't deal with people very well, but we had other strengths. I am writing this book on a Saturday morning, listening to Enya's music, and the words flow through my fingers into the screen as fast as I can type. This is fun for me. This is my bliss. I know to seek out what gives me joy, for that marks my path, in life. The thought of helping teenagers seek out their joy, as they develop their mission and purpose in life, and improve their communities, fills me with energy.

Sure, people still think I'm weird. They also know me to be generous, kind, and encouraging. You make a living by what you get. You make a life by what you give. I give all I can, in fun ways. OK, so I'm not perfect. Perfection is a process, not a product. I thought I was "damaged goods", in high school. I realize now that I was an ugly duckling, among chickens [the original version of that story] and that I was intended for something greater, in two worlds- land and water.

IV. Things to be aware of

There are really only two choices in life. They are kindness, and violence. These are based in love, or unity consciousness, and fear, or separation consciousness. I have found that kindness is a lot more fun.

Here is how I see it. Let us imagine that we are a planet, circling around a Sun. When we face the Sun, the light, there is nothing to fear, for what we see is light. When we face away from the light, we see shadows, which can perhaps be fearful. Seeing the light in people is fun, because it gets stronger, as we notice it. I have seen the best in people for a while, and they bask in it, they love it. Seeing what is bad in people is not as useful, though one does need to be aware of it at times.

I mentioned the *Hsin Hsin Ming*, before. I plan to write a rhyming verse version of it- for fun. Its main point is to stay out of judgment. I would add to stay in the question.

Here is why it is useful to stay out of judgement. You can really only understand numbers, and judgments, in comparison. What does 42 mean? I have no idea. 42 what? Oh, 42 ways to be more aware, as opposed to 41, or 43. Ok, now I have a comparison. We could call this a gradient- which might be rising, as in 41, 42, 43, or falling, as in 43, 42, 41.

Comparisons have a gradient. Think about the story of *Brer [Brother] Rabbit and the Tar Baby*. Brer Rabbit finds a tar baby, and bitterly resents not being treated with the respect he thinks he deserves. Notice that- he compares what happens, which the way he thinks it should be. From the Comparison, he moves to Resentment, Resistance, and Revenge. This is the cycle of violence, and it can run in under one second of clock time.

This is a traditional African teaching story, which brings this cycle into conscious awareness, so it can be stopped.

You will find people who have poisoned themselves with resentment. In the jungles of India, fruit falls from the trees, and may fall into puddles. It can ferment, into something alcoholic. Elephants, when they have this "jungle juice", get crazy, just as crazy as someone drunk on resentment. Some people are so full of resentment, that you might want to avoid them. Sometimes it is possible to help them drain this.

How do you know which to do? Well, listen to your gut, your intuition. Some people think men don't have intuition. I read histories of men that survived combat. Note that- survived. Those who didn't survive didn't write books. Those who did survive ALWAYS say something like they felt a feeling that told them to move, they did so, and a few minutes later an artillery round fell right where they were before.

One book, written by a WW II veteran of the European campaign, noted that he was being targeted by German machine-gunners. Something happened, and not only did he see in 360°, he also saw through the eyes of the machine-gunners, he knew where they were going to fire, and he was able to evade their fire. He lived to write the book. Of course that's impossible, yet it happened to him. Then again, we haven't even begun tapping the potential of all that is in the mind, so maybe multi-Dimensional perception might be possible.

You subconscious mind has a Prime Directive to keep you alive. It usually doesn't speak in language; it speaks the language of symbol, sign, dream, hunch, or feeling. IF YOU LISTEN to these, it will guide to you what is useful, and steer you away from what is not useful.

Those are usually the only two judgments that are useful.

Whatever is <u>useful</u> to you is what gives you joy, expands you, helps you grow, encourages you, builds you up, and gets the job done.

What is <u>not useful</u> to you is what disheartens you, constricts your growth, discourages you, tears you down, and does not get the job done. Though this may be useful, for some larger goal. Context is important. I am not saying that the unpleasant parts of life are not useful. They can be. My military service was at times unpleasant. However, I learned a lot.

There will be people you will need to avoid. Perhaps they are so poisoned with resentment that you cannot reason with them, and they may cause harm. Perhaps they are simply so far lost in darkness that you can't get them out. Your gut will tell you, as it does for everybody, who has done great things.

Having said that, how do successful people get the information, and resources, that they need? The answer is very simple. They ASK FOR IT. They open their mouths and ask.

Many people would like to do more good in their community- and their time is limited. They might have a spare skill saw, or wood, or a connection, or something else that would be useful to you, in your goal. If they like you, and like your goal, they may well just give it to you, to see something good done. Always end your questioning with this: "Who else do you know, who could help me?"

When you ask people for help, always <u>clearly define exactly what you seek</u>, BEFORE you ask. If you need help for an hour or two, on a Saturday morning, they might say yes. If you ask for an open-ended commitment, this means you didn't do your homework, and they will say no. Clarity creates.

What happens, when they say no? In my area, they have insurance salespeople called the "tigers". They will actually thank people who say "no" to them. Why? Because they know they have to get 60 "no's" before they can get to the "yes". Rejection just propels you to the next opportunity.

Let's say you approached that magnificent woman, or guy, and they really cut you by not only having no interest in being with you, they even insult you. Oh, does that hurt, right? Yeah. For about 3 seconds, until you say, "NEXT!" That is the magic word. Hey, there is rejection in life. So what? The journey of a thousand miles starts with the first step, and continues step by step. So you completed a step, and you move on to the next step.

And for those people who cut you up emotionally… the best revenge is to live well, following your joy. I guarantee you that people who harm others like that are not following their joy, they are drunk on resentment, and they hate their lives, though they will never show this to you.

It is easy enough to hold onto resentment. The problem is that it is poisonous. There was a guy in high school who did me great damage, with malice aforethought. He died of cancer, about seven years ago. I would not have wished that on him. He created it for himself. He kept his habit of causing harm.

There was one lass in high school, who seemed to think it was her duty to harass me. I just stayed away from her. I know from class reunions that she can't hold a relationship together, she's too toxic. Part of her stress and trauma management program is consumption of alcohol. Her picture on Facebook shows the kind of face I've only seen in people taking cortisone, it's really puffy.

A guy on the bus I ride to work told me about a lass he really, really liked, in high school, but had no interest in him. He is so very glad he's not involved with her now. Between drugs, and alcohol, and similar not-useful behaviors, she is a wreck, now.

My nephew told me, when he was in high school, that the popular, "in" crowd, was very shallow and superficial. I said, "well, and you are perceptive." I have met many women who were never invited to be with the "in" crowd, in school, so when they grew up, they created the "in" group, so they didn't have that problem. Nia Vardalos shows this in her Big Fat Greek Wedding movies. It's real. I have far more joy in my life, than anybody who was in the "in" group in my high school.

Pain is part of life. Pain is the feeling of weakness, and lack of awareness, leaving the body. Pain is a very patient teacher, which taught me some lessons I could learn no other way. I'm not saying I welcome pain, however I do remember the lessons she taught me, very well.

Rejection is just another stepping stone on the path to success. There are no mistakes, there is no rejection, there is only learning, and persistence.

Poisonous people are teachers, as much as any addict. They clearly mark paths that you will not want to be on. Thank them for their valuable teaching.

A Native American told me once that the Creator apparently wanted him to learn a lot of patience, because the Creator seemed to have filled his world with people whose only purpose seemed to be to help him develop his patience. Oddly enough, the Creator seems to have the same program for me. Perhaps you have some of this program yourself. Welcome the teachings. Life is a school, full of learnings for those who choose to be aware, ask intelligent questions, and pay attention when the answers show up.

After my father passed on, I wrote a book about his life, for my daughter. I realized that he had said a great number of proverbs, or maxims, or sayings. I further realized that these had come to him from his own ancestors, and that these refined bits of wisdom were often very useful. I read books of proverbs, even in foreign languages. They are fascinating wisdom.

Here is one from Arabic: fatish an il-um, wa tazawaj min bintiha, which means "seek the mother [you want to be married to in 20 years], and marry her daughter [for she will be like her mother, in 20 years]. Here are some in English:

Marry in haste, repent at leisure.
Three may keep a secret, if two of them are dead.
One kind word warms the heart all winter [Kurdish].
Fall down seven times, get up eight times [Japanese].

Smart people *pay attention to detail, pattern, and process*. I told my older daughter, when she was 14, that I wanted to meet her first serious boyfriend, so I could see a younger version of myself. She said, angrily, "Dad, I will never qn@lw!entn2bdkem!" I met her husband, not long ago. He was doing the same job I did, at his age, in the same place, he was quiet, he read a lot of science fiction, and he was… a lot like me.

There is a flow, in human affairs. When you pay careful attention to that flow, whole new sets of possibilities open up. You realize that you can accomplish much more than you thought possible. People start helping you, because they like what you're doing, and want to support it. Sometimes you won't even know who helped you; the help will just show up.

It will seem as if the Universe is helping you, every step of the way. It did for me. I welcome it, though it never shows up when or how I expect it to.

V. Do it now

Don't wait for leaders. <u>Do it now</u>- person to person.
-Mother Theresa

Planning is useful. Things get done, though, when you take action. Taking action is very simple. Your generative questions have opened up your perception, so that you see what needs to be done. Here is the magical secret:

DO IT NOW.

Don't wait. Don't wait till your plan is perfect. Don't wait till you have all your ducks in a row. Don't wait until you have all the data you need. Don't wait till the funding is in place. Just… do it. Now. Uses of Funds, in your plan, is always more important than Sources of Funds.

I was on a committee that created a small park, totally with volunteers, in Granville, MA, at the corner of Routes 189 and 57. The land was donated to the town, on the condition that a park be created, at no cost to the town. People showed up. Two old houses were torn down, by volunteers. The field stone in the basement walls was taken out.

A guy in town had a small bulldozer. He got dirt and filled in the basements. Topsoil was obtained. He spread it. Gravel was obtained, and a bed and backing of gravel was used, with the low stone walls. I helped with the stone walls. I lent my books on Japanese gardens to the woman who did the design. There are benches, areas for shady and sunny gardening, granite curbstones, and it looks great- it is the kind of place people do weddings at, in June.

They followed the rule of "Do it now", within the critical path limitations of course. You don't put a roof on until the walls are mostly done.

There is a soup kitchen, not far from where I work. I take socks, and warm hats and gloves in winter, new shoes when I can get them cheaply, and other such things. Of course it's not a lot. However, the staff there are so delighted to see one guy who shows up every now and then, with stuff. It is worth it to me, to bring stuff, just to see the joy on their faces.

Perhaps the single most important reason to do it now, is that other people will notice. Some of them will really like what you are doing, and support your efforts, here and there.

Here is an example. I sometimes get my hands on used clothing. I pass it on to a church-based outfit, that puts the clothing out on tables, for people to take, in troubled areas of the city I work in. I'm told it never takes more than five minutes, for the clothing to be gone, once it is put out.

Sometimes people at work give me clothes their children have outgrown, or other things. Given this interest, sometimes events happen that take me right to places where I can get resources to help people. Having the focused interest means that I notice things, details, events, and patterns that I wouldn't otherwise notice. It feels like I live in magical Universe, at times- and this is specifically, and only, due to my focus, which is shaped by my questions.

Focus is incredibly important.

VI. Sales theory for leaders: leaders "sell" ideas/visions

If I designed high school curriculums, I would require a course on sales theory, and theater. Sales and theater skills are something people use every day, in a job. I loved geometry, and calculus. I haven't used either since college. I use sales theory every day.

Consider dealing with your parents. If you really want them to buy a book for you- relate it to your education. My daughter did her third year of college, in Italy, in Italian. She told me she needed the Harry Potter books in Italian, and also the books on CD-ROM, to learn Italian. The only question I asked was, "and what address did you need that sent to?". She knew her education was extremely important to me.

You say you aren't selling, in school. Aha. Yes you are. Teachers LIVE for that student that does more than the bare minimum, in the class, the student that asks intelligent questions, the student that seeks. They took up teaching because they loved their subject. When you look at that boring math textbook… what did it take for the authors to write it? Great fascination with the subject. Your teacher dedicated his/her life to their subject, so they could share what they loved with students. That don't care...

If your teacher assigns 11 new words to learn, in Spanish, learn 15. I figured this out late in college, I wish someone had told me in high school. My nephew picked up on it, though. I told him to stay one unit ahead, in math. They always tell you the easy way to solve the problem, in the next chapter. Since he had read the next chapter, he knew the easy way to solve the problem. He was offered a full scholarship at Umass Amherst, and later a stipend and free tuition to get his M.S. there. They paid him to get his Master's degree. How does it get better than that?

I asked my father how he could take 25 college credits per term, and work full time. He said he always showed up to class, and would ask the professor if he could turn papers in early. Nobody ever asked that before.

I took a language course at the Defense Language Institute, a military language school. I stayed five chapters ahead of the class, and learned extra dictionary words. The teachers were astounded. It wasn't hard. I just got five chapters ahead, and then it took no more work to stay ahead than normal.

In a class for my Master's degree, I had to write a paper. I read some of the prof's papers, and learned his biases, and what he believed to be true. So I wrote my paper, proving what he believed to be true, using sources he had never heard of. Guess what the grade was. Yep, I maxed it.

Why do this? Well, for one reason, it's fun. Another reason is that guess who writes the recommendation letters for you, to get into college, or even for an employer? The time to sell them on writing a good letter is not when you need it. It is when you are in their class. They will remember you.

Here's another reason to do this, especially in college. A friend of mine in high school spent all of his money from his job on college graduate level math textbooks. He read them, and did all the problems. He maxed the SATs, with a 1600, the max at that time. He got a full scholarship to Princeton, and now does classified research for the Navy. He's in his dream job.

You see, teachers, and professors, know about opportunities that they don't tell the class about. But they do share news about this with those students that show promise, those that have "sold" them, on how good a student they are. Why not? It feels really good to "feed" interest, and who wants to waste their time on those who have no interest in a gift?

Sometimes, employers will go to a professor, and ask which students shows incredible promise. Or, the professor may know of a very special employment opportunity, or scholarship. Guess which students they share this information with?

A year of high school education in the U.S. costs between $5,000/year, and $10,000/year. Are you giving/did you give good value, for that investment? If I had known what I know now, in high school, I would have asked many, many more questions than I did.

My brother worked for a company with a CAD/CAM program, for electronics manufacturing. He did on-site trainings. He could turn a $100,000 sale into a $250,000 sale, in about 45 minutes, and have an absolutely delighted client. How did he do that? He did his homework. He knew what problems the clients had, he knew his own company's offerings, and he would show them how his company's offerings helped them solve their problems, effectively. Clients loved him.

What do they pay you to do, in most if not all jobs? To _solve problems_. Usually, the bigger the problem solved, they more they pay you. Many employers pay close attention to community service, and hobbies, on resumes. People involved in community service are generally very focused, capable of managing their time well, they ask intelligent questions, they solve problems, and they aren't wasting time in addictions. Most people are very good at their hobbies.

I actually don't know how to talk to people, beyond the basics. So I ask how someone who is really good at it would speak. Then I speak that way. Theater skills can be very useful this way.

Everything about you- your appearance, your command of the language, your attitude, your energy level, the way you walk, all of it is "selling" you, every moment of the day.

I am a veteran, of the U.S. Army. It was not easy, though it was far, far easier than it was for my father's generation, during WW II. We actually got six hours sleep per night, in basic training. During my father's time, they would wake up recruits at night to go running, do close order drill, and otherwise mess with their heads. One learns to get by on less sleep, in the military.

Even there, every day is a "sale". When I was in, spit polish wasn't allowed on boots, nor were uniforms starched any more. Still, they demanded that we look a certain way, and always, always, always, have a clean shave. To this day, I can't go out of the house, without shaving. I can do wilderness stuff without bathing, but in "civilization", I have to be clean.

An animal that doesn't take care of its fur, or appearance, is usually sick. You can't judge a book by its cover, of course, yet for most people, appearances are all they know. I knew a guy in college who showed up to job interviews in grossly inappropriate clothing. Oddly enough, he didn't get the jobs.

Don't dress for the job you have. <u>Dress for the next level up</u>. Don't limit yourself to the activities for the job you have. Finish those, quickly, and learn and do what you need for the next level. Do you remember my high school friend, who was studying college graduate level math textbooks? Do you suppose that might have helped his college applications? It did. A lot.

A friend of mine has a 14 year old daughter, who wants to be a doctor. I found some cool medical dictionaries cheap, using booksalefinder.com, and gave my buddy these, for his daughter. I told her that if she mastered just one page per day, in a year, she'd have 365 pages of stuff mastered- and a major jump on other students. PLUS, her college entrance essays would have this clear evidence of major focus, on her goal. Wanna guess she'll do well on her MCATs, the exams to get into med school?

VII. Imagination- feeling and observing it real

There is a skill that all millionaires use, though not all are conscious of it. Here is how I use it. This is basically training your nervous system in success, not failure. This is useful.

A. I find myself a place I won't be disturbed. Sitting is usually better.
B. I breathe deeply, for a few minutes.
C. I relax into wide angle vision, where I can see 180°.
D. I look up at a 30° angle.
E. I let all the tension out of my body, with each outbreath.
F. I imagine a scene that could only occur if my goal was already real, as I look through my own [imaginary] eyes, hear through my own ears, and feel in my body. It could be the sound of my brother on the telephone, excitedly telling me about his new job. It could be getting some award, at work. The key point is that my goals helps more people than just me, and causes no harm.
G. Each time I do this, I notice some new detail.
H. In time, the event comes to being in the real world.

Observation is powerful. A friend of mine in Virginia moved into an apartment, that had bare walls. He put up skiing posters, though he'd never skiied in his life. Within six months, his daughter paid for a ski vacation to Colorado, where he learned how to ski.

A Native American elder told me once that our eyes eat images, the way our mouths eat food, and we become what we eat. If you aren't controlling the images, sounds, and feelings in your body, someone else is. That someone else might not have your best interests at heart. The Mass Media has one goal: to sell you products. Their goal is not to educate you, help you, or to in any way benefit you. Most of their revenue comes from companies that pay them to sell you their stuff.

Would you pay a garbage company to dump a load of garbage into your living room? Seriously, would you? I wouldn't. Yet watching the mass media is about the same thing. They make you feel bad, and inadequate, so you'll buy more stuff to "fix" it.

The images, sounds, words, and feelings that you feed into your deeper mind create your world. When you look at your world, and see shortcomings, know that these were programmed.

A leader changes the input, and so, gets much better output. A leader realizes that you can't shave your beard by putting the razor to the mirror. You have to work on your inner mind first, if you seek changes in the outer world, which really only mirrors what is going on inside you.

Another way to say this, is that what you imagine, you create. If you imagine yourself separate from creation, and powerless, you will be. If you imagine- observe- yourself part of creation, with power that comes as you set useful goals, you will be.

Many of life's greatest realizations are extremely simple. This is the simplest one I know of. Maybe that's why it seems to be difficult for some people, who feel justified blaming circumstance, and other people, for their problems.

The sequence you see here is a very simple one. It cost me 45 years of seeking, to get the awareness to put it this simply. Neville Goddard's talks, on youtube.com, or his books, discuss this. So do the books and talks of every other successful personal development course, from Wallace Wattles to Tony Robbins.

Choices choose futures. I don't know if what I imagine creates my reality. However, I have tried it out, as a theory, and it works for me. I find reference to this in every sacred book I've ever looked at, and also in all personal development books I've read.

VIII. When you're really stuck

In 1995, after my second divorce, from an alcoholic, I realized that I just wasn't clear. So I did a four day Vision Quest. Native Americans put their teenaged boys on these, so they would get the crap out of their systems early, and know what they were on the planet to do[2]. I was older, 35. The land was carefully chosen, as not having had trauma for a while. I did bring water, as I am a "civilized" person. I had no food, and no distractions. I kept my mind empty, and it was like nothing happened the first day. I felt sick, on the second and third days.

I stayed in a roughly 10 ft/3m square. Once per day, I walked about 40 yds/m to the path, and left a rock there. The groundskeeper would come by, to check the rock, to be sure I was ok. I had a military entrenching tool, for feces. I had four gallons of water. I had a sleeping bag, and clothing.

On the fourth day, the dam broke. A flood of awareness broke through, on many levels. It was like a massive download of useful energy, a mother lode of awareness. I still cannot put most of it in words, because I can only model about 10% of my experience, in language. I so very much wish I'd had this gift when I was a teenager. But now was all I had to work with.

I went back to work. Somehow, writing was a lot easier. I "knew", somehow, what to do, to get things done. A beginner in the Martial Arts strikes many blows. The advanced student needs to only strike one blow, for he pays attention to the flow, and knows when to act. The master, however, doesn't need to strike any blows. The master has enough awareness of the flow, that he redirects himself, and/or it, so that blows aren't necessary. I was at the advanced student stage.

---

2 Traditionally, women only very rarely did Vision Quests, but nowadays more and more are. I spoke with a woman last week who had done one. Some native people bitterly resent theft of their culture. The Visionquest is worldwide, however. Jesus, Muhammad, Orpheus, the Zoroasters, and many others did them.

Nick Hockings, an elder of the Ojibwa people, and Navy veteran, who lived at the Lac du Flambeau reservation, told me that I didn't have to do the full quest. Here is my understanding of his 24 hour quest sequence, which, as he said, is used worldwide- from Catholic retreats, to Buddhist monasteries, to Sufi exercises, to cultures that still live very close to nature.

A. Identify a room, in your house, where you won't be disturbed for 24 hours. Remove or hide all distractions. A closet might work. An attic might work.

B. Identify a question you need answered, which could be "What is my mission and purpose in life?", or "How do I accomplish this next phase of my plan?". It needs to be an important question, where the answer would be useful, and help more people than just you. Obsess on this question. Ask it a number of times, perhaps 72, or 108, with heartfelt knowing that as you ask, it is answered.

C. It would be good to start fasting the night before, that is, don't eat food, or if you do, make it very small amounts, and avoid meat, alcohol, drugs, sugar, artificial sweeteners, and junk food. Limit intake to fresh, raw fruits, vegetables, grains, nuts, seeds, and sprouts, with maybe fresh fruit or vegetable juice.

D. Drink pure water. Have one glass of water, that you drink half of. Say to yourself, just before sleep, "When I wake up, I will have the answer to my question". Go to sleep, asking the question, and imagining how you would feel, if it were already answered. Be aware of your dreams.

E. You make wake up with the answer. If not, simply spend the day, in the room, with no distractions. When thoughts come up, reshape them to your question. How would you feel, if you had the answer? Drink only pure water.

F. Go to sleep, asking the question.

G. You will wake up with an answer. It will probably not be the answer you expected, and you may not even recognize that you got an answer at first. Pay attention. It is there. It may show up in events during the day.

IX. One major piece to be aware of

Community service may involve taking some risks, in approaching people. Here is a very simple rule: if, when you scan someone, they feel bad, don't approach them. Here is an example. My younger daughter is on the autistic spectrum. She loves to go up to total strangers, and greet them cheerfully. We were in a restaurant, once. She gave a wide berth to one guy, at a table. I thought that was odd. I scanned the guy, myself.

He felt like a hit-man [assassin]. I knew I was also going to give him a wide berth, in fact, I wasn't going to come back to that restaurant ever again. I didn't need any confirmation, I didn't need rational proof, I didn't need anything more than that feeling. Maybe it was wrong. I don't care. I learned something in the Army- listen to my gut. When it tells me what to do, I do it, without question. Most men, however, do not know how to do this.

I take risks, in community service, for one reason, aside from helping- I have a well-developed intuition. Zen masters in Japan taught spacial awareness. They would sneak up behind students, and hit them with a stick, until the students learned to feel behind them. That is how I learned it, metaphorically, in the Army.

There is a reason you see more women involved in community service than men. It's a bit sad, but it is very real. I was a Boy Scout. I talked to a guy who was also a Boy Scout, who greatly enjoyed it. I asked why he wasn't a Scoutmaster. He looked at me seriously, and said, calmly, "I have a family, kids, a life, and a mortgage. One accusation, and it all blows up."

When I was a lad, accusations against adults, by teenagers, were sometimes ignored, and sometimes followed up on. Nowadays, accusations against adults are handled the way the Office of the Holy Inquisition handled things. There is really only one defense- stay out of the minefield. Would you risk your life, your ability to support your family, your mortgage, and to eventually get whatever pension there is, on unstable people who could cause you great harm? You wouldn't.

Most men won't, either. I have to pass the civilian equivalent of a Secret security clearance, every year, because I handle large amounts of money, at work. Do you really think I'm going to take any risks, around that? The answer is no.

So how do you deal with this? Talk to other people first, especially women who are close to that man. Find out his interests. Many men would be quite happy to help out in some way that they can, safely, especially if they can give through an intermediary, or "cut-out".

I have given around 100 used sewing machines, to a small organization that passes them on to women who cannot afford to buy them, in the last 16 years or so. I have given carloads of used clothing, shoes, toys, sports equipment, dishes, silverware, cooking utensils, and other such stuff, to this same program. I was happy to do it.

I don't do it directly- I have a "cutout". I pass them on to a guy I know, who gets the material to people who can pass it on directly to those who need it. I have a wife, an adult daughter, and a young autistic daughter. I minimize my risk. I am happy to help others- when it feels safe to me.

Approaching people through intermediaries often get better results. In Spain, people ask intermediaries what their boy/girlfriend really thinks about them. People can be more honest through intermediaries, and feelings don't get hurt, as much. Using intermediaries used to be much more common, in our culture. Leaders work with intermediaries, aka matchmakers.

X. One community service anybody can do today

The Wampanoag [Algonkian, or Aninishnabe] elder Manitonquat [Medicine Story] writes books on how to heal communities. I went to one course he taught. He asked us to pair off. One of us would be the "Listener". Listeners were to listen with the body language of total attention.   Listeners were to say nothing, maintain eye contact, and at most say "hmmmm". The other was the "Speaker".   Speakers were to talk about whatever was bothering them, what they were proud of, or anything they had a lot of emotion on. This was simple.

So we began. About five minutes after I started speaking, it was like a core dump of all my frustrations and resentments came out, not so much in words, but in feelings. It was like a roto-rooter for my heart. OK, this sounds odd, but that's what it felt like. I felt a very strong sense of community, with the Listener, it's hard to explain. We were in a high state of rapport.

This same process can occur in the military. WW II veterans used to say that they never got as close to people, as they did with their buddies in the War.   This is not a surprise; we have no real mechanism in our culture, to dump out no longer useful feelings.

That is unfortunate.   Instead, people self-medicate, and pursue addictions, instead. I have a small group of people that I meet with by conference call, on the weekend, and we help each other.

A long time ago, I was working a midnight shift, in a hospital. I was getting residency in the state, to cut my tuition.   I was depressed, not eating well. I mentioned before that some have told me I match the Asperger's syndrome profile. I don't know, but it could be. I didn't know how to deal with people, then, beyond very routine communication. I was very depressed.

There was a woman there, who simply let me talk. I knew up front there would never be anything between us, but she did let me talk. I was of course always respectful. She allowed me to make the mistakes that most people make in their early teens, in learning how to communicate. What I learned from her was and still is a critical part of the body of awareness and experience I use to communicate with people today.

Looking back, had I been her, I would not have taken the risks she did. Young men are perhaps not always stable, or trustworthy. Yet she did take the risks. I am forever in her debt. I will never be able to repay her for her kindness. I haven't spoken to her, in many years.

The only thing I can do, is to of course pay it forward, that is, to pass her kindness on to others. I do so, at every opportunity. People pass on what they get- whether it is kindness, or violence. Most people don't think, they are on automatic pilot, and simply pass on what they get, and imitate others.

Decisions have consequences. Which will you choose, today? Violence, or kindness? Violent people live in fear. Kind people live in love, the all-encompassing love.

Real leaders choose that path that serves the greater whole.

I have found that kindness is a lot more fun.

XI. Some useful questions

What would I like to create, in this world, if I had no limitations[3]?

What blessings would I like to leave behind, when I graduate from my time in this world?

What questions might I ask, where as the answers show up, I get closer and closer to my goals?

How can I be so cheerful, and positive, that negative people just go away?

How can I detach from the energy drains, and connect more to the energy chargers?

How could I have fun, putting joy in people's hearts?

How does it get much better than this?

How is this useful to me?

How much better can it get?

How would I feel, when my life is better than the best I can imagine?

How would this feel, real, now?

What gives me joy? How can I find joy in everything I do?

What other wonderful stuff could happen?

---

3 It would be useful to post questions like these in your bedroom, and ask them daily, to help focus your day.

Where is the flow, and how can it help me achieve my goals?

How does it feel, as I realize that the Universe wants to help me create all these wonderful outcomes?

How does it feel, to be one with all that is, and benefitting the whole, with my dreams, choices, and actions, as the Universe helps me?

The conscious mind can handle 6-8 pieces of information at a time, which is why phone numbers are 7 digits long. The subconscious mind can handle 60 million pieces of information per second, that they know about.

When you ask questions like the above, you open yourself up to a stream of useful information and awareness.

I wonder how else you could have fun playing this incredibly useful tool?

I wonder what kind of changes you would enjoy making, in your world, with this tool?

I wonder how you have already shifted yourself to a much more powerful state, just by contemplating these points?

I wonder how your perspectives have changed, and integrated, as you contemplated all this, and what new possibilities just opened up for you?

I wonder just how much fun, joy, peace, contentment, satisfaction, love, happiness, and all that makes life worthwhile, you could experience, just be asking questions like the above?

What is the maximum amount of fun a person could have? What would it be like to exceed that, I wonder?

When you are sufficiently "on fire" with the beauty of your Vision of what is possible, when you are totally committed to it, when you live, breathe, and eat your Vision, it gets so much easier to "sell" it to others.

How could your Vision of the possible be even more exciting?

What else could you notice about it, that would get your energy to a high level?

The slave trade in the British Empire was halted by four people, who got together, and asked questions just like these.

Your parents didn't have to pay for your school textbooks directly. This idea came from one guy- Huey P. Long, governor of Lousiana. He further had the revolutionary idea that black children should also get schoolbooks, in the same way- this in the American South of the 1930's.

The German Enigma coding machine was broken first by Polish military people, who passed it on to the British. Alan Turing devised the first electronic computers, to assist in breaking Nazi codes, during WW II.

The electrical devices you use, that operate on Alternating Current [AC], all go back to the 20 patents that Nicola Tesla filed. He could design a machine in his head, run it for thousands of hours in his imagination, and then, take the parts apart, to examine them for wear- in his imagination. He had a plan to broadcast free electricity world-wide. He also created the first microphone, which he gave to Marconi, and the first robot-controlled boat.

I wonder what you could have fun creating, to benefit humanity, and our world?

71399346R00026

Made in the USA
Columbia, SC
27 May 2017